P9-CLU-534

BETTER BY SATURDAY™ DRIVING

Books in the series

BETTER BY SATURDAY DRIVING

BETTER BY SATURDAY IRON PLAY/LONG GAME

BETTER BY SATURDAY PUTTING

BETTER BY SATURDAY SHORT GAME

BETTER BY SATURDAY™

DRIVING

Featuring Tips by
GOLF MAGAZINE®'s
Top 100 Teachers
with Greg Midland

WARNER BOOKS

NEW YORK BOSTON

Warner Books

Time Warner Book Group
1271 Avenue of the Americas, New York, NY 10020
Visit our Web site at www.twbookmark.com.

Printed in the United States of America
First Printing: May 2004
10 9 8 7 6 5 4 3 2 1

Library of Congress Cataloging-in-Publication Data
Midland, Greg.
Better by Saturday—driving : featuring tips by Golf magazine's top 100 teachers / Greg Midland.
p. cm.
ISBN 0-446-53257-6
1. Golf—Drive. I. Title.
GV979.D74M53 2004
796.352'3—dc21 2003010619

Book design by HRoberts Design

CONTENTS

Foreword: Better by *When?*

When I heard the concept of this new series of books, "Better by Saturday," my reaction was immediate: "Hey, it's already Friday." But having seen the series, I'm convinced that the promise of its premise is fulfilled in these pages, which feature some of the best instruction you'll find in a month of Sundays.

If you're like many golf lovers I know, you dream of playing every day, try to play every week, and settle for a bit less than that. An occasional eighteen is better than nothing, but with so much time between rounds, it's tough to groove a swing. How can your muscles remember the inside-out path they took to the ball when you hit that huge drive your last time out? How can you hope to improve, knowing that PGA Tour pros pummel hundreds and even thousands of practice balls for every one you hit?

Here's how. This book contains the best, simplest tips we could get from the game's finest teaching pros, GOLF MAGAZINE's Top 100 Teachers. They work with thousands of ordinary golfers every week, as well as with top amateurs and Tour pros. They are the best in the business. And thanks to our

Top 100 Teachers, each of the four books in the Better by Saturday series—they cover driving; iron play and the long game; the short game; and putting—is full of advice that will help you play better your next time out. You don't have to change your swing. Just pay attention. It's easy, since these tips are clear and often entertaining. Even golfers who play every day will learn plenty.

It's all here: everything from teeing a ball up to hitting one off hardpan or out of a tough lie in a fairway bunker. If there's a situation or shot that always ruins your score, you'll find the cure in these pages. If your troubles take a new form every time out, you'll still find ways to shoot a lower score this weekend. And after that, you can re-read this volume for further improvement, or pick up another of our "Better by Saturday" books.

Imagine how good you might get by next month.

Kevin Cook
Editor, GOLF MAGAZINE

Acknowledgments

Many thanks to Mike Malaska and the staff and members of Superstition Golf & Country Club in Superstition Mountain, Arizona, who gave photographer Fred Vuich and me full access to their two gorgeous Jack Nicklaus–designed courses. Also thanks to David Huffman and Gary Newkirk for their patience and diligence in helping us to produce the photographs. Finally, thanks to all of GOLF MAGAZINE's Top 100 Teachers, present and past, for the book's most important element: the tips. ***—Greg Midland***

BETTER BY SATURDAY DRIVING

Introduction

Watch Tiger Woods, Ernie Els, John Daly, and scores of other pros rip a drive down the fairway, and one word comes to mind: wow. Seen up close, it's just pure, unadulterated power. That "wow" factor is what we all play for.

It's why today's elite golfers are hitting the weights like never before. It's why golf equipment companies are continually searching for the right mix of materials and technology to build the latest, longest drivers. It's the sly smile that comes to your face when your tee shot flies past those of your buddies.

Of course, savvy golfers know that crushing the ball 300 yards doesn't mean much if you can't hit it reasonably straight. Most tour pros would not trade 10 yards of added length if it meant being 10 yards less accurate. It's this combination of distance and accuracy—total driving, as defined by PGA Tour statistics—that is the holy grail of everyone who plays this game.

Excluding the par-3 holes, you typically have 14 chances each time you play to tee off for maximum distance. Out of 80, or 90, or 100 total strokes, that's well below 20 percent of your total game. But driving is important because it sets the tone for the entire hole. A good tee shot not only instills confidence, but allows you to attack the hole the way it was designed. That's the route to lower scores.

The question is, how do you become a better driver by Saturday? There are no shortcuts, but chances are you can improve your performance with minor adjustments, not major reconstruction.

GOLF MAGAZINE's Top 100 Teachers know how to communicate these nuggets of wisdom to all types of golfers, from aspiring beginners to accomplished professionals. The tips in this book are ones you can do quickly and easily.

Each tip is boiled down to its essential meaning, and organized by subject. They run the gamut from preswing grip checks to power boosts in the backswing to post-impact keys for accuracy, from quick drills to strategy to stretching the key golf muscles.

As a group, they are sure to add more "wow" to your tee shots.

CHAPTER 1: PRESWING

Start with Ease

Use a swing trigger to release tension before the takeaway

Tension often builds before you take the club back, reducing the amount of clubhead speed you can generate. A swing trigger can help ease you into the backswing.

If you tend to stall over the ball, try the lower-body move used for many years by Gary Player. At address, kick your right knee gently toward the target before starting the takeaway. This trigger promotes a solid weight shift to the right foot during the backswing, and gives you a feel for the ideal impact position—the right knee releasing inward and weight shifting back to the left foot. Try to avoid a forward press involving the hands, because there is always a danger of twisting the clubface away from a square address position. ***—Johnny Myers***

Ball Position

A slice can come from the ball being too far forward

Many "banana ball" slicers position the ball too far forward (opposite their left toe) at address [photo 1]. This forces the shoulders to start open (pointing left of the target), promoting an out-to-in swing path and a slice. Instead, the ball should be in line with your left armpit [photo 2].

To check your ball position, grip a driver and take your address. Lift the club straight up: If it is perpendicular to your body, your ball position is correct. If the club is angled so that the clubhead is out in front of the grip, the ball is too far forward. Correct yourself by bringing the club perpendicular to your body, then lowering it straight down. That's where you should play the ball. ***—Mike Adams***

1
2

Squeeze Out Tension

Tighten your hands briefly to counteract tension

The hands and arms must be relaxed to make a smooth, free-flowing swing that is easy to repeat and produces solid, powerful contact. When tension rises, the resulting swing is almost certain to be choppy and quick, because the muscles in your hands and arms are too tight.

The easiest way to relieve this tension is by giving the club a quick, tight squeeze as you address the ball, then releasing. Going from a very tight grip to a softer one releases some pressure; you can actually feel the tension leaving your upper body. Now you'll be ready to swing the club back as smoothly and rhythmically as possible. ***—Peggy Kirk Bell***

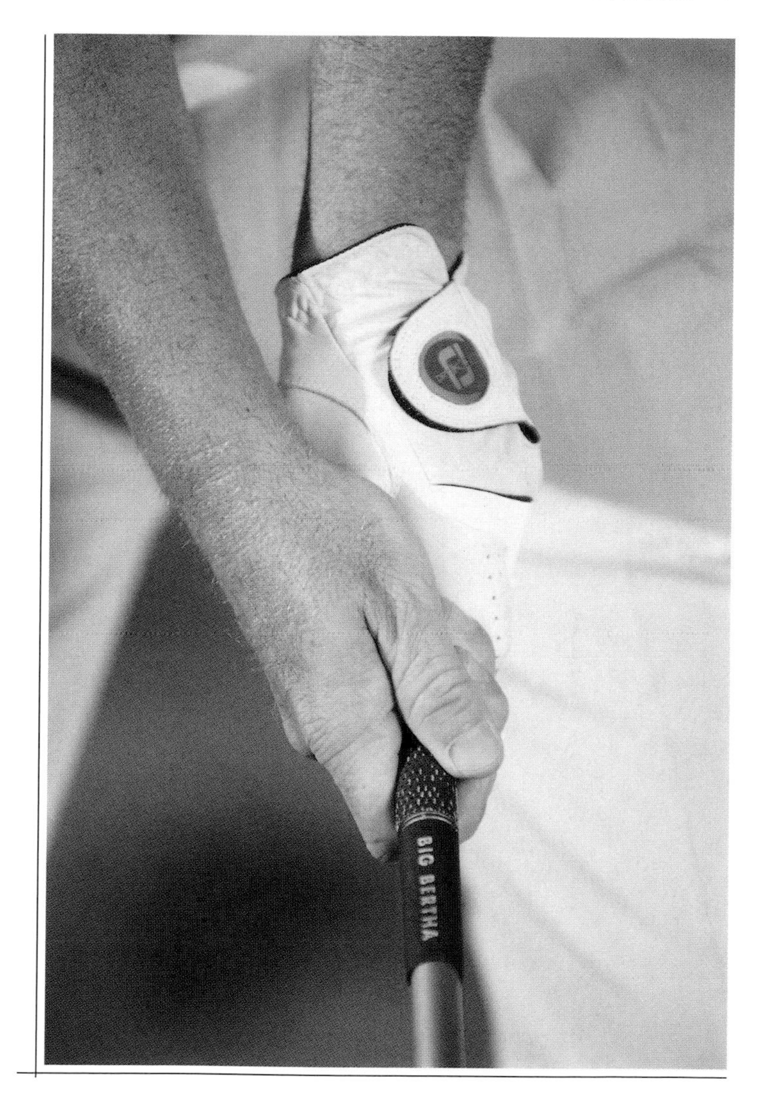
BIG BERTHA

Relaxed but Ready

Feel how the right posture can turn into a powerful swing

How you stand at address affects how you swing. In order for your arms and body to move freely during the swing to maximize clubhead speed, you must start from a relaxed, well-balanced posture at address.

The next time you're preparing to tee off, picture yourself in a ready, athletic address posture. Your stance should be sturdy and your upper body should feel reactive, as though you could catch a medicine ball without losing your balance. This solid foundation serves as the basis for any good swing. ***—Bill Davis***

QUICK TIP

Tee It High

To hit longer drives, tee the ball high and make contact above the clubhead's center of gravity. If you're hitting the ball high on the face, the bottom of the clubhead will contact the tee. As a drill, line up several tees in a row—with no balls—and practice hitting the tees without hitting the ground. You want to make the tee flip up in the air, a sign that you've maximized power. *—Keith Lyford*

Higher and Longer

Get your head behind the ball from the beginning

To hit your drives with more carry, and therefore more distance, you should be behind the ball at impact so you can catch it on the upswing. But it's not easy to get behind something you weren't behind to start with.

To get and stay behind the ball, take your normal driver stance, then move your right foot a step away from the target, so your feet remain square to the target line but wider apart. This foot shuffle places your head farther behind the ball. See for yourself by setting up in front of a mirror and shifting your right foot. Watch your head move back to where it belongs. ***—Butch Harmon***

Address with the Heel

Use the rubber-band effect to stop your slice swing path

When you swing over the top, the club approaches the ball from out to in and often leads to a slice. You can stop swinging over the top by stretching your arms like a rubber band.

Take your address with the clubhead centered behind the ball. After your last waggle, push the club away from your body by stretching your arms out. The ball should now be lined up at the heel of the club. From this position, make your normal backswing. At the top, your arms will retract and the club will drop, like a rubber band being stretched and then released. This will help you deliver the clubhead to the ball from inside the target line, a path that promotes a powerful right-to-left draw. ***—Bob Hamrich***

Eyes on Plane

Swivel your head at address when looking at the target

The shoulders tend to follow the eyes, so if the eyes remain parallel to the shaft plane through impact, the shoulders will also be on plane. This increases your chances of making solid contact for the longest, most accurate drives.

At address, be aware of the proper path of the clubhead away from and back to the ball. Then set your eyes roughly parallel to this path. Keep your eyes on this plane by swiveling your head, rather than raising your head up, when you look at the target. This will help keep your eyes, and therefore your shoulders, on plane throughout the swing. ***—Michael Hebron***

Set the Right Hand

Avoid a slice setup by delivering a square right hand from the side

Most people are right-hand dominant and put too much of their right hand on top of the grip, instead of on the side. Gripping on top pulls your right shoulder forward, shifting the shoulders open to the target line. This sets you up to cut across the ball and hit a slice.

You can prevent this by adopting a simple grip procedure. First, sole the clubhead and grip the club with your left hand. Then, bring your right hand in from the side, making it difficult to place your hand too high on the grip. With the right hand in the right place, you can align the clubface and your body correctly. ***—Craig Shankland***

Club Height

The club should point at the belt buckle for a good takeaway

The height of the hands at address is critical: If they are too low, the wrists will cock the club up too steeply; too high, and the forearms will rotate the club too far inside. Both faults lead to inconsistent contact and missed fairways.

To ensure correct hand height, check that the butt of the club is pointing at your belt buckle at address. A proper address can correct swing errors before they happen, especially in the takeaway, and help you drive the ball straighter and longer.

—Peter Krause

Hover the Club

Go through your regular preshot routine and, at the last moment, raise the driver off the ground so the center of the clubface lines up with the ball's equator. Hovering the club increases your awareness of the clubhead and promotes a smooth, tension-free start and a free-loading windup on the backswing. Now you're ready to rip it.—*Joe Thiel*

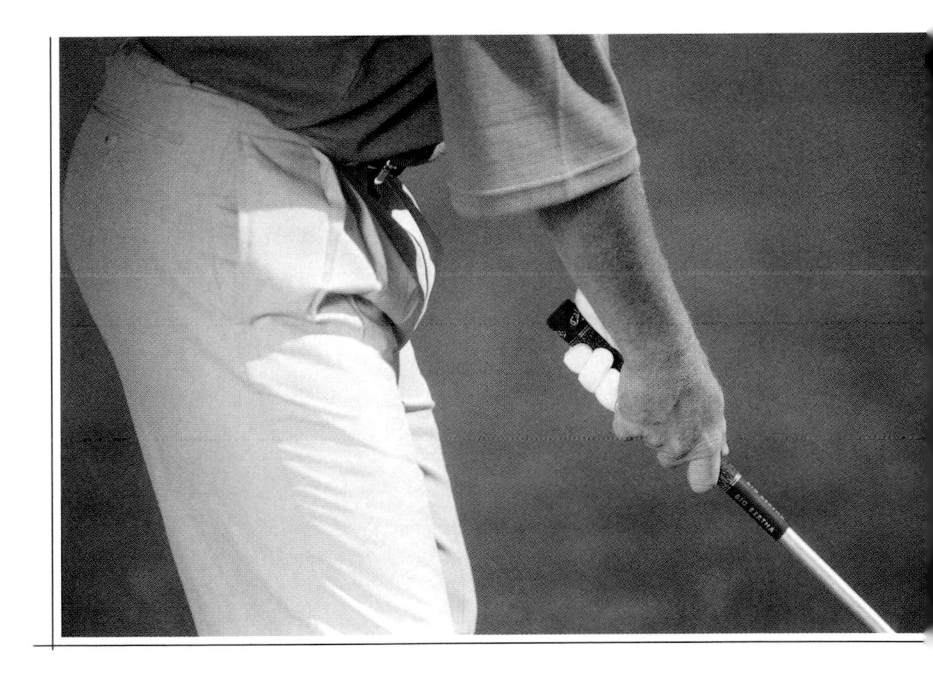
BIG BERTHA

See Your Grip

Trust your eyes to help you get the right grip every time

The chief cause of a golfer's inconsistency is variation in grip position, often so small a change that the player isn't aware it has occurred. Avoid this by placing your hands on the club by sight, rather than feel.

As you take your grip, raise the club out in front of you and use your eyes to check the exact alignment of your left, then right hand. Rather than relying on how your hands feel, which can vary depending on factors such as temperature and humidity, the key is to memorize the exact visual details of your completed grip. Use these references each time you grip the club, and you'll avoid a major hidden cause of a slump. ***—Manuel de la Torre***

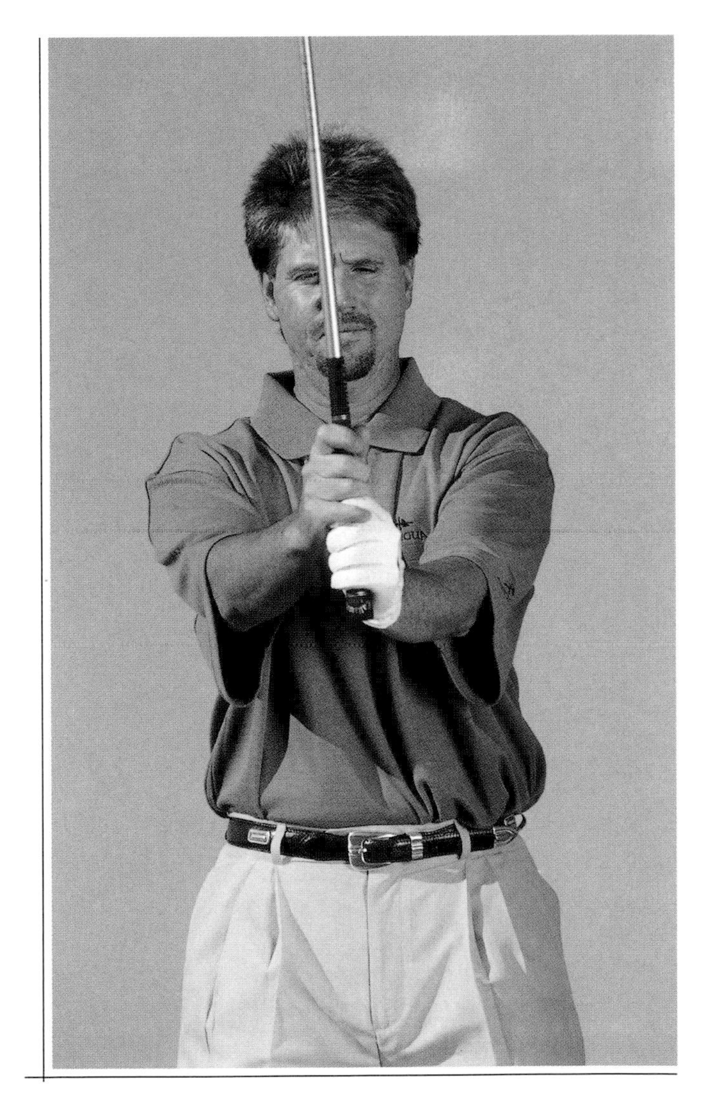

Leg Drive

Set more weight on your back leg at address to hit the ball long

Much like a home run hitter in baseball, the golfer seeking more distance from his tee shots must make a lateral leg drive through impact. The best way to encourage this move is to set more of your weight behind the ball at address.

Think "heavier on the rear leg, lighter on the front leg." Many amateurs do just the opposite and lean toward the target, resembling a batter getting ready to bunt. Setting more weight on your rear leg at the start lessens the need to shift much weight there before starting the downswing. In effect, it presets the leg thrust, which can add up to 20 percent more distance to your drives. ***—Eddie Merrins***

QUICK TIP

Stay Target-Focused

Getting "ball-bound" is a major source of tension, which prevents you from making a free-flowing swing. Take a cue from Tour players and spend more time looking down the target line than staring at the ball. Remember, study the target line, and glance at the ball. *—Jim Flick*

CHAPTER 2: POWER

Wind Your Body

Let the big muscles of the upper body build a powerful backswing

Long hitters share a common trait: backswings that allow the back, chest, and shoulders to stretch and build resistance against the more stable lower body. This differential is a big-time power source that any player, even one whose backswings stop short of parallel, can achieve.

Keep the left heel planted and let the hips pivot back to a comfortable position in the backswing. Even if your club is short of parallel at the top, you'll get plenty of distance because your upper-body muscles are stretched into a full coil. On the downswing, think about unwinding these same muscles to produce the added clubhead speed you're looking for. ***—David Glenz***

Right at the Top

Form an "L" with your right arm to maximize swing arc

The signatures of a powerful swing include a wide, powerful arc and a shallow clubhead angle into impact. Some of the game's longest hitters achieve this by focusing on the motion of the right arm.

Try to form an "L" with your right arm at the top of the backswing. This will widen your swing arc, which is helpful because a narrow arc reduces clubhead speed and steepens the club's angle of attack, increasing the likelihood of a slice. Depending on your degree of flexibility, you may or may not be able to reach a perfect 90-degree bend in the right elbow. But striving for an "L" will activate your right side and widen your swing arc so you can hit the ball longer. ***—Kevin Walker***

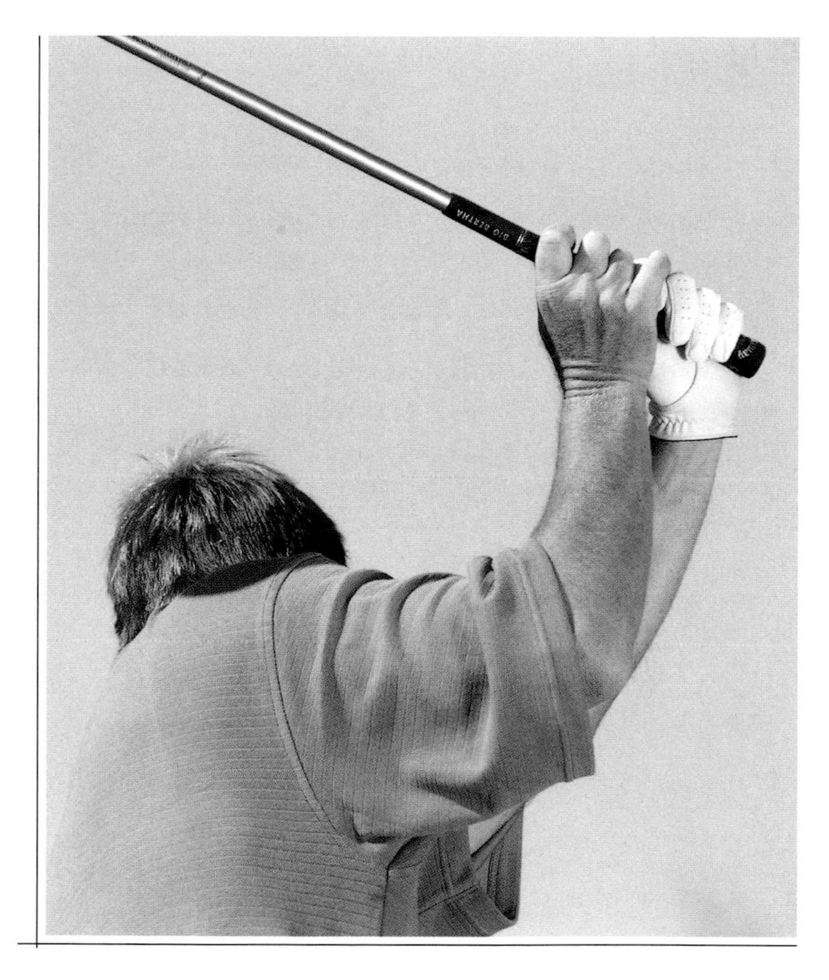
BIG BERTHA

Straight Arm

A downswing key to help you boost distance

A common cause of short drives is jutting the right shoulder out instead of down at the start of the downswing. Power is lost as the club comes over the top and approaches the ball from a weak, out-to-in swing path.

To put some punch back in your tee shots, start straightening your right arm before you reach impact. This move positions the right shoulder behind the left, letting you swing powerfully down the line through the ball. The club will swing into the ball from the inside on a vastly improved swing path. As you reach the post-impact position, the right arm will be fully extended as the club swings around to the finish. ***—Fred Griffin***

QUICK TIP

Swing Past Impact

Don't try to hit at the ball, but rather swing well past it. This mental key prevents you from decelerating the club in the impact zone. Instead, you'll make a tension-free motion, accelerating the club so it is traveling at maximum speed when it meets the ball. ***—Jack Lumpkin***

Club Acceleration

Think "gradual descent" to build speed through the ball

Are you looking for more distance? Violence is not the answer. Too many amateurs try to create distance by either pulling the hands down quickly or lurching toward the target with the upper body. Both moves rob the swing of its power key—the gradual acceleration of the club on the downswing. One way to groove a more gradual descent is by maintaining your head position until after impact. Learn to do this by hitting balls with your feet together [photos 1, 2, and 3]. From this stance, you can't move the head forward on the downswing without losing your balance. Keeping your head behind the ball allows your lower body to unwind and pull your arms through impact, creating the gradual acceleration needed for distance. ***—Dick Tiddy***

1
2
3

A Bigger Hip Turn

Move your right foot back at address to let the hips move freely

A strong hip turn, free-swinging arms, and a good weight transfer are all speed generators that result from corresponding moves in the backswing. If you have trouble building power in the backswing, try the following technique to get the feel of a complete turn.

At address, move your right foot farther away from the target line and flare it slightly outward. This moves the back leg and hip out of the way, creating more room for hip rotation. The more the hips rotate in the backswing, the more they will rotate in the forward swing, allowing the arms to accelerate through impact.

—Kent Cayce

Maximum Coil

Sit on a chair to feel how the lower body supports the coil

The body coil is the swing's engine: The muscles wind up on the backswing and uncoil on the downswing, sending the clubhead to the ball with maximum energy. A good coil is one in which the upper body turns and lower body resists, so that your hips turn only half as much as your shoulders.

To feel a proper coil, sit on a chair and lean your upper body about 30 degrees forward. Grip a club as you normally would and start your swing by rotating your left shoulder toward your chin. You'll feel the large muscles of your back stretch; once you do, you've reached a full coil. Translate this feeling to your swing and let the lower body lead the uncoiling during the downswing, which will launch the ball farther with less effort. ***—Carl Lohren***

Stay Flexed

Key on the right knee to stay in posture and hit the ball longer

If you're looking to flex a little more muscle off the tee, keep your right knee flexed throughout the backswing. A flexed knee encourages turning against the right leg, creating a level shoulder turn and a big, wide windup. Straightening the right knee causes the arms to swing up and tilt the spine toward the target—a reverse pivot.

As you swing back, sustain the feeling of pressure on the inside of your right knee. Feel as if your weight is shifting to your right heel as your arms bring the club to the top. Keeping this knee flexed will allow you to make a full shoulder coil without letting your spine tilt toward the target. ***—Dick Farley***

More Extension

How a better wrist cock can plug a major power leak

A major flaw of most amateurs' swings is an early wrist cock. This occurs when the hands lift the club up on the takeaway, causing the swing to become steep and preventing the weight from transferring to the right side. Without this "loading" going back, your body can't "unload" for power on the downswing.

Avoid this early wrist cock by making a wide extension on the takeaway. When the hands get to hip height on the backswing, the clubhead should be at the same height, not cocked straight up in the air. This gets the upper body turning behind the ball sooner, which naturally transfers weight to the right side. From here, you can shift forward to start the downswing with power. ***—Rick Grayson***

Wide Backswing

Use the lifeline of your right hand to create leverage

The more you extend your arms during the backswing and the longer they remain extended in the downswing, the farther you'll hit the ball. To create this leverage, your angle of attack has to be elliptical—like an egg lying on its side—rather than steep.

To set up a wide backswing, push the lifeline of your right hand against your left thumb. This squeezing, combined with the backswing, pulls your arms and club away from the target and widens your arc. Try to maintain this pressure on the downswing to set up a powerful arm swing through the ball. ***—Phil Ritson***

QUICK TIP

Even Timing

Your backswing and your forward swing should take the same amount of time. Try counting "one-thousand-one" as you swing to the top, then again from the top of the swing to the finish. Since the forward swing is twice as long as the backswing, it has to be twice as fast. Try to make the fastest point of your swing at impact to enjoy better contact and increased distance. *—Rick McCord*

Knuckles to Ground

The movement of your left hand boosts clubhead speed

Rotating the knuckles of the left hand to the ground through impact is a major power generator. Not only does it square the clubface for a more direct hit, it dramatically boosts clubhead speed by signaling a good release.

Focus on twisting your left hand down as the clubhead approaches the ball, as if you were turning a key. Try this exercise to get the feeling: Hold your left wrist with your right hand and practice swinging the club from halfway down through the hitting area [photo 1]. The isolated movement of your left hand slings the clubhead forward and rotates your knuckles to the ground [photo 2]. ***—Robert Baker***

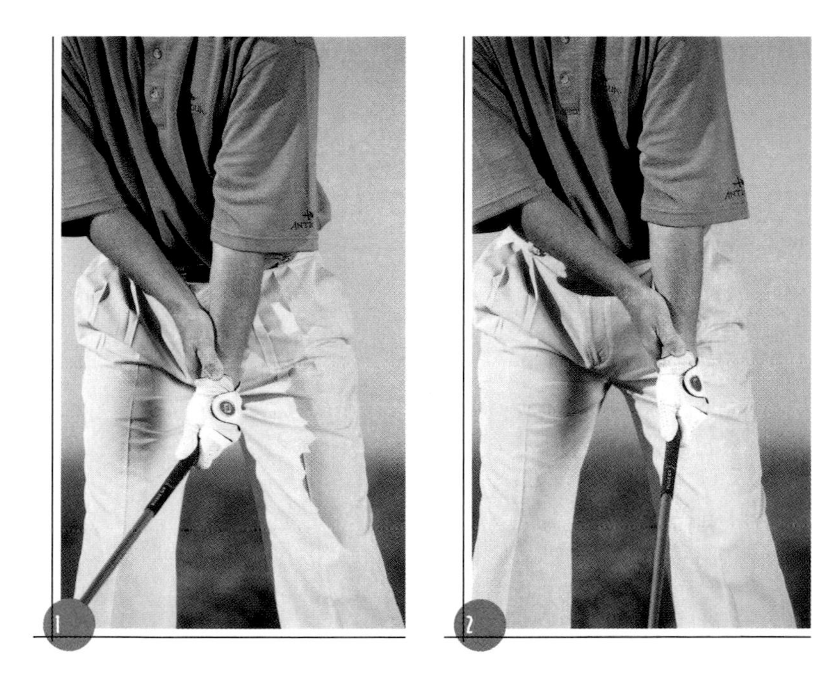

Shoulder Turn

For the best path back to the ball, turn the shoulders 90 degrees

The shoulders must stop turning at a 90-degree angle to the target line—no more, no less. At this point, the arms have a direct path back to the ball, allowing you to hit the ball longer with a shorter, more relaxed swing. Check your shoulder turn by holding a club across the front of your shoulders. Swing back until the club is at a right angle to your stance line. Depending on your flexibility, you may need to either open or close your stance to stop at 90 degrees; just ensure that after making this adjustment, your clubface is still aimed square to the target. ***—Rick Martino***

CHAPTER 3: ACCURACY

Flatten Your Swing

Feel the club swinging around the body rather than up and down

Most slicers swing more steeply than they should. This comes from moving the arms mostly up and down, rather than around the body. If you swing around your body correctly, you should be able to leave behind the weakest shot in golf.

Instead, imagine a baseball swing, noting the way the arms rotate around the torso. Try not to let your hands rise above your head at any point during the swing. This around-the-body motion will help you create the sensation that the clubface is pointing down to the ground after impact. ***—Bill Harmon***

The Right Arc

Keep the club on the target line longer by moving the right elbow

In the early part of your backswing, let your right elbow swing away from your side to get your club moving on the optimal swing arc. This will add width to the arc and boost clubhead speed, but it is just as important for keeping those long shots in the fairway.

When your right arm separates, you can keep the clubhead on the target line longer, helping to start it on the correct path to the top. When your left arm reaches parallel to the ground, your path and plane will be correct if the club feels light and balanced above your hands and the butt end points between the stance line and the target line. You'll make a backswing that produces straighter shots. ***—Darrell Kestner***

Draws and Fades

Work the ball both ways by altering your spine angle at address

It's true that hitting draws and fades requires different swing paths, but that doesn't mean two different swings. By adjusting your spine angle at address, you can make these changes occur automatically.

Think of a "normal" posture angle as 20 degrees of tilt, though it varies from player to player. To hit a draw, reduce your forward bend at address, to about 10 degrees [photo 1]. This posture promotes a flatter backswing, encouraging the slight inside-to-outside clubhead path that produces a draw. For a fade, bend your spine forward to about 30 degrees [photo 2]. This promotes a more upright backswing that increases the ability to cut across the ball from outside to in. ***—Bill Davis***

1
2

Aim, Then Align

Get the right preswing sequence to hit shots to your target

Aiming and aligning are separate tasks. You aim the clubface, then you align your body parallel to that target line. Most amateurs, especially slicers, get this order wrong and end up aimed well right of their target. Holding the club in your right hand only, place the clubhead behind the ball and aim its face at your target. Then complete your grip without moving the clubhead. Next, place your toes parallel to this target line, and finally align your knees, hips, and shoulders parallel as well. Follow this sequence every time, even in practice, and the improved setup position will help you hit more fairways. ***—John Gerring***

QUICK TIP

Hip Motion

Imagine you're a batter trying to hit the pitch over second base. At the start of the downswing, the hips should shift toward first base. From there, they will uncoil naturally, pointing toward second when the club is approaching the ball, and then toward shortstop at impact. You can encourage the correct hip motion by trying to hit the inside of the golf ball. *—Harry "Lighthorse" Cooper*

Stay Coiled

Keep the shoulders in check on the downswing

Most poor contact comes from the shoulders turning too soon on the downswing, causing the upper body to lunge toward the target and shifting the bottom of the swing arc in that direction. If your goal is also to eliminate a slice, the good news is that making more solid contact usually causes the slice to disappear.

When the upper body takes control, the club comes into the ball too steeply and produces left-to-right slice spin. Try to keep the shoulders coiled as the lower body unwinds to lead the downswing. This sequence sets up a solid, level angle of attack, with your sternum just behind the ball—not lunging forward—at impact. ***—Donald Crawley***

Smooth Takeaway

Start the swing with the club and body in rhythm

Done correctly, the club and body start the backswing together, with the wrists cocking gradually as the clubhead gains momentum. If one or the other takes the lead, the rhythm of the swing and the path of the clubhead are both altered, leading to mis-hits.

Focus on starting with a rhythmic motion in your preswing. Use a waggle to keep the body from freezing before the club starts back. As you're ready to go, make your last waggle flow seamlessly into the takeaway. This action will keep your muscles relaxed and smooth out the transition to the takeaway, ensuring that the arms, body, and club are synchronized. ***—Gary Smith***

Train Your Left Arm

Imagine bowling a strike on the backswing

A slice may be born at impact, but it's often conceived in the backswing. Too often, the slicer swings his arms abruptly to the inside, rolling the back of the left hand to the sky and turning the clubface wide open. This usually causes an outside-to-in swing path that produces a slice.

Here's a great image to help you feel the correct movement in your left arm. Assume your address position and imagine a bowling alley directly to your right. Without moving your feet, feel like you're rolling a strike with your left hand, curling the ball in from the left gutter [photo 1]. Your hand and arm will swing upward with a slight rotation of the forearm [photo 2], precisely the motion you should feel in the backswing. ***—Peter Krause***

1
2

Tilt Away from the Target

Maintain your spine tilt through the swing

The common mistake among inconsistent ball strikers is to lean the upper spine toward the target at address. This weakens the grip, sends the clubhead outside the target line, and leads to a reverse weight shift—a combination that robs power and creates a slice.

Start by setting the proper spine tilt at address, and maintain it all the way to the top of the backswing. This fundamental is vital for consistency for three main reasons: It encourages the club to approach the ball from the inside; it initiates a proper weight shift to the right foot on the backswing; and it keeps the upper body behind the ball at impact. All of these benefits are crucial for driving the ball with consistency. ***—Bill Moretti***

Down the Line

Temper an out-of-control hook by swinging the arms to the left

Getting a case of the duck-hooks is no fun, but it can be tamed. The culprit is a severe inside-to-out swing path, the exact opposite of a slice. Keep your swing more fluid and improve your path by focusing on the motion of the arms after impact. Rather than swinging them out to the right, think about moving the arms left and across the body into the finish. For the slicer, this is not a suggested move. But if you're hooking the ball, swinging the arms to the left will promote upper-body rotation through impact, delivering the clubhead down the target line. ***—Mike McGetrick***

QUICK TIP

Fix a Slice

To cure a slice, picture a clock painted on the ground with the target line running through the "12" and "6," and the ball in the middle. Feel as if you're swinging from 7 o'clock to l o'clock to help fix an outside-to-in swing path. In reality, the clubhead will never reach 1 o'clock, but this image will help straighten out your ball flight. *—Bob Toski*

Perfect Your Pivot

How to easily achieve a better pivot on the backswing

Rather than turning the hips, many golfers shift them laterally. This is known as swaying, which ruins your posture and takes away both power and consistency.

Understand that you're trying to pivot around the base of the spine. The key to stability, and a powerful coil of the weight around the right side, is creating resistance in the lower body to prevent the hips from swaying. While swinging to the top, maintain the angle of the right leg established at address—tilted slightly toward the target. While straightening this leg leads to a sway, holding this angle keeps your weight over the inside of the right foot and encourages the perfect pivot. ***—Rob Akins***

CHAPTER 4: STRATEGY

Windy Driving

A plan to handle tee shots into the wind

If wind gusts are strong, your expectations off the tee must be readjusted. Still, you want to give yourself a chance, which comes in the form of a low drive that doesn't balloon into the teeth of the breeze.

For solid contact and a lower trajectory, you want to maximize your body's stability and make a shorter swing. Widen your stance a couple of inches and grip down one to two inches on the club [photo 1]. This will narrow your swing arc and give you more control. Also, tee the ball lower, so that less than half of it is above the top of the club [photo 2]. Resist the temptation to rush the swing. Make the motion smooth and rhythmic. ***—Laird Small***

1
2

Wise Waggle

A technique to make your preswing waggle really count

A good takeaway leads to a good swing, so why not develop a waggle that programs this feeling? This has a double benefit: It reduces tension in the arms and also gives you a preview of the right takeaway path. Place a club on the ground positioned from your left heel across your right big toe. Grip your driver and gently swing the entire club (not just the clubhead) back from the ball. Done correctly, the club in your hands will be in line with the club on the ground. Now try to duplicate this feeling to start your swing. ***—Bill Moretti***

Stop Steering

Worrying about trouble on one side of the hole will cause you to steer away from it, sometimes so far that the ball lands in trouble on the other side. Stay committed to your target by aiming your club at an intermediate spot along the ground, such as a divot or patch of discolored grass. This practice is much easier than aiming at a spot well down the fairway, helping you to make an uninhibited swing and stop steering the ball. *—Kevin Walker*

First-Tee Jitters

Tips to perform your best on the opening tee shot

Every golfer has experienced anxiety as they step onto the tee to start a round. This first tee shot is often called the most important swing of the day, and it can affect your confidence for the entire round.

The first step to combating this nervousness is to lighten up, and remember it's only one of 18 tee shot swings you'll make. Craft a plan for the shot and stick to it. If your opponent just hit a mammoth tee shot and you'd like to incorporate something you saw in his swing, now is not the time to do it. Zero in on your target and determine what type of shot you should play, then visualize the ball landing in the fairway. ***—Rick McCord***

The Low Stinger

Hit more fairways by learning how to play a low tee shot

When teeing off to a tight fairway, sometimes a low, controlled shot can be the best play. This "stinger" is hit when the left wrist is bowed at impact, meaning it is firm and curved toward the target [photo 1].

To feel this, hit punch shots with a long iron and practice the "hit and stop," where you abbreviate the swing right after impact [photo 2]. The only way to do this is to keep the left wrist firm. Start small and work your way up. Begin by hitting 5-iron punch shots about 30 yards off a tee, then gradually add distance by extending the length of your swing. Once you have the feeling of the bowed left wrist at impact, the stinger can be one of the most reliable shots in your bag. ***—Craig Harmon***

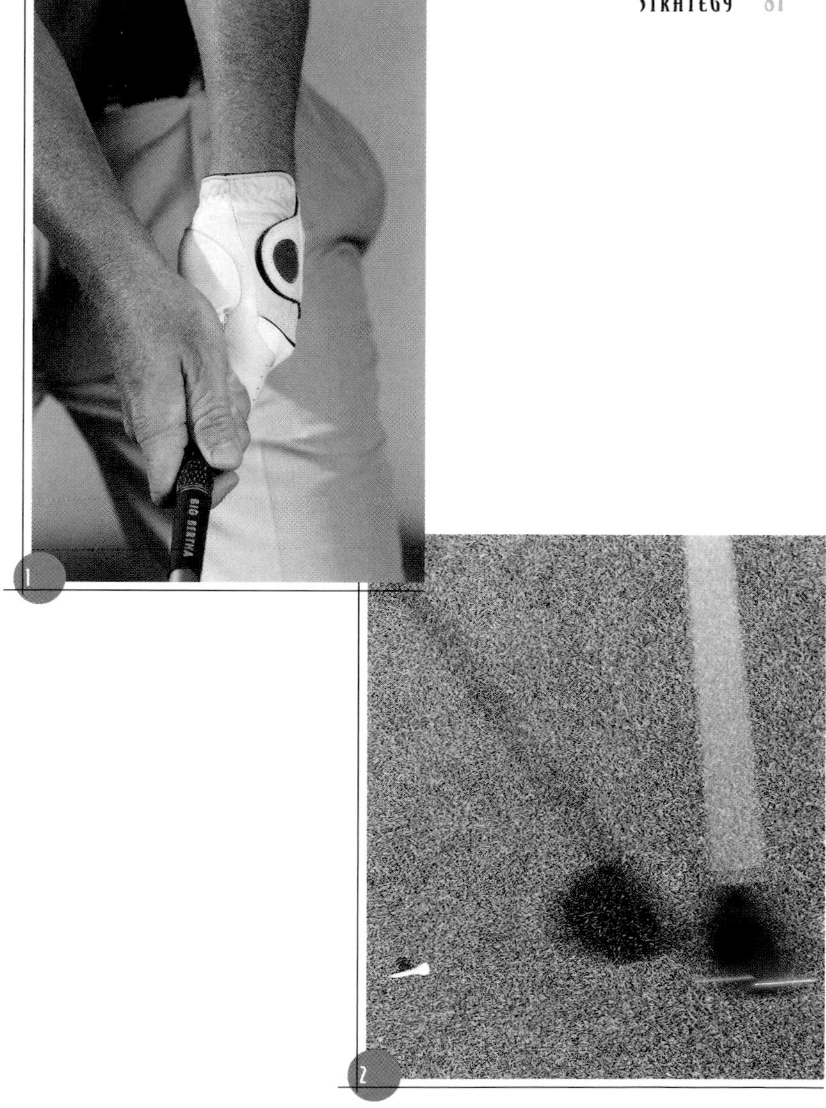
BIG BERTHA
1
2

Dogleg Dangers

When to change your strategy on tight doglegs

Your number one priority on dogleg holes should be hitting the fairway. This is especially true if the hole doesn't fit your prevailing shot pattern (e.g., your fade on a dogleg left).

When a hole curves away from your usual shot shape, hit a fairway wood off the tee, aiming away from any bunkers or hazards guarding the corner of the dogleg. This is much better than hitting with a driver and trying for a marginally longer shot that might finish in a poor position. By hitting a more lofted club, you'll have a longer approach shot to the green, but it's a better option than approaching from the rough or sand. ***—Mitchell Spearman***

Aim the Ball First

Line up the ball's logo to help with alignment

You've seen the Tour pros line up putts on the green with the ball's logo or other identifying mark. Take a cue from their strategy and carry this technique to the tee, the only other place where you have control over placement of the ball.

Since hitting more fairways has as much to do with proper aim as it does with your swing, it makes sense to do all you can to ensure you're prepared to hit the ball where you want. Crouch down behind the ball and line up its logo so it points straight down the target line. You can aim the clubface perpendicular to the logo, and then align the feet and body parallel to this line. It is a great aid, so use it whenever you can. ***—Rick Martino***

Fairway or Bust

Use the tee markers to your advantage under pressure

Late in a match or on a very tough hole, driving the ball in the fairway is a must. You need a comfortable "go-to" shot you can call up under pressure. If your natural ball flight is left to right, tee the ball up on the far right side of the tee box and hit your baby fade down the fairway.

Placing the tee near the right tee marker—or near the left marker if hitting a right-to-left shot—increases the chances the ball will curve back into the middle of the fairway. It forces you to aim farther left than you might otherwise, playing right into the hands of your dominant shot. ***—Gerald McCullagh***

QUICK TIP

Those Extra Few

When you want a little extra yardage, try going against your instincts. Instead of thinking you have to swing at 125 percent, aim at a point in the fairway that's about 75 percent of your maximum distance. This will relax your muscles and free up your swing. You'll probably blow it past what you thought was your maximum. *—Dr. Richard Coop*

When to Hit 3-Wood

Three situations when keeping your driver in the bag is a good idea

Hitting the 3-wood off the tee isn't a sacrifice; it's smart golf. Its shorter shaft and additional loft make it easier to control than the driver, so you'll hit more fairways. Here are some situations when the 3-wood should be your choice off the tee.

- **Driving with the wind:** The ball gets launched higher than with a driver, meaning you might get added distance while keeping the ball in play.
- **Long par 5s:** You can't reach the green in two anyway, and the 3-wood will make your lay-up positions easier by helping you hit the fairway to begin with.
- **Swing trouble:** When you don't have your "A" game, hit the 3-wood to regain some confidence. ***—Mike McGetrick***

1
2
3

CHAPTER 5: DRILLS

Turn Like a Windmill

Feel how your arms and shoulders turn in relation to your spine

Moving up and down during the swing can be detrimental to solid contact. Understand that your turn must be perpendicular to your spine angle, not to the horizon.

To feel this, first stand upright with your arms straight out to your sides. Keeping your arms extended, bend from the hips as if you were addressing a golf ball and turn like a windmill by rotating your upper body back, then through. Notice that the left hand is lower on the backswing, while the right hand is lower on the throughswing. This shows you are turning around your spine, keeping a constant posture throughout the swing. ***—Derek Hardy***

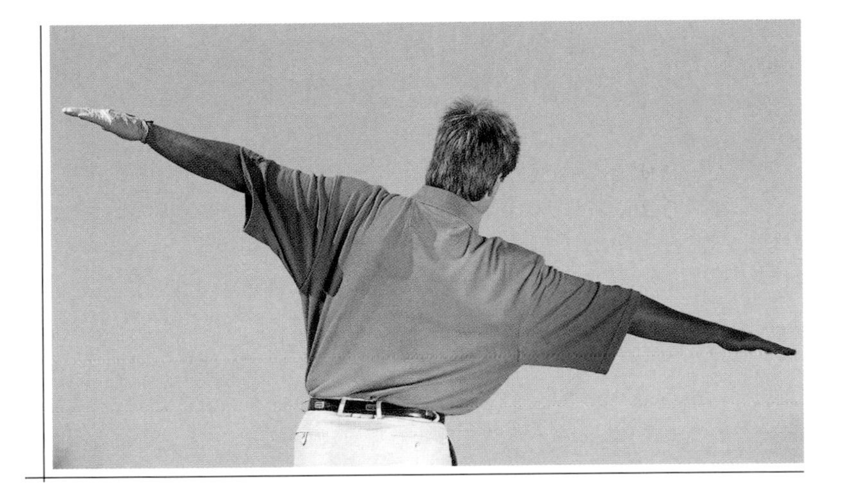

Backward Drill

Turn your back to the target to feel an anti-slice release

Golfers who slice would love to turn their backs on that ugly banana ball. Here's a drill to do just that.

With the ball on a tee, set up with a 3-wood. Keeping the clubface square to the target, close your body until your back almost faces the target. Making the best swing you can, hit 20 shots this way. Starting so far from square forces you to keep the arms and club turning through the downswing, which is a great release key for every long swing. Now return to your normal address position and hit another 20 shots. You should find it easier to turn through the shot and square the clubface at impact, and you may start hitting draws right away. ***—Butch Harmon***

Center-Face Contact

Swing through the gate to hit the club's sweetspot

To see where on the clubface you are striking the ball, try the "gate" drill. Address a ball with your driver and then stick a tee in the ground one inch outside both the heel and the toe. Your objective is to swing through the gate without hitting either tee.

If you clip the inside tee, you are making contact on the toe. Since this often results from tension, concentrate on keeping the arms relaxed coming down and extending them fully through impact. If you clip the outside tee, you are making contact on the heel. This signals an outside-to-in swing path; try making practice swings releasing the right hand at the start of the downswing to let the left arm lead the club on the proper path. ***—Gary Wiren***

Full-Body Release

Feel how the arms swing in sync with the body for more power

Use the full-body-release drill to ingrain how the club and arms should rotate in front of the body on the downswing and stay in front until after impact. This keeps the arms from racing ahead of the body and causing errant drives.

Place the butt end of the club into your sternum and slide your hands down the shaft until your arms are extended. Note the triangle formed by your arms and chest. Keeping this triangle intact, swing back and through. This will help you deliver the clubface to the ball squarely, and backed by the power of your entire body. ***—Jimmy Ballard***

Brush the Logo

Use the logo on your shirt to train your arms

Most mis-hits are born in the backswing, as the arms get out of position and move the club on a poor plane. Try this drill to get the sensation of the correct arm motion to set your club in the best possible position at the top.

Grip an iron in your left hand only and grasp your left wrist with your right hand. Swing the club to the top, brushing the logo on the left chest of your golf shirt with the inside of your left arm. Imagine the logo is a piece of wood and you have sandpaper under your arm: You want to smooth the wood with the sandpaper. This teaches the proper upward movement of the hands and arms, encouraging a straight path from the top through impact. ***—Robert Baker***

Better Balance

The "dance drill" grooves a more balanced weight shift

Balance is crucial to long drives and solid contact. To feel where your balance should be at the top of the swing and at the finish, dance your way through this drill.

Swing the club to the top and lift your left foot off the ground, balancing your weight over your right leg [photo 1]. Then step through and swing to the finish, lifting your right foot off the ground as your body rotates through [photo 2]. Your weight should now be over your left leg. If you can do this without losing a step, you know what it feels like to be balanced at both ends of the swing. ***—Lynn Marriott***

1

2

The Finish

Strive for an "I" finish position for better body rotation

Watch most Tour pros today and you'll see that their left sides at the finish are in a straight line from the foot to the shoulder, forming an "I." This position signals an aggressive trunk rotation through the ball and allows for a swing that produces longer drives.

Feel the right finish position by teeing up a ball and taking your normal address with a 9-iron. Now take your left hand off the club and, with the right arm only, swing back and through the ball to the finish. If you maintain good balance, you'll make solid contact and your upper body will rotate properly all the way to the "I" finish. ***—Gary Smith***

QUICK TIP

Half Motion, Full Speed

You need to pay special attention to your swing pace, especially in the first move down, in order to let the club build momentum. This drill should help you build awareness of your speed: Tee up your driver and hit the ball with a full swing, but only half the distance. Without the urge to generate power, you'll make a smooth transition to the downswing and synchronize your arms, body, and club. ***—Jim Flick***

Pull for Power

The left shoulder can open the door to increased distance

Long drives come from making a full rotation on the through-swing, led by the left shoulder pulling away from the chin. At the finish, your right shoulder should be closer to the target than anything else.

To feel how the left shoulder initiates the power pull, hold a mid-iron across your upper back and shoulder blades and get into a good setup. Then simulate a backswing by pulling the club with your left hand until your back faces the target. Now for the key move: Push the club back toward the target with the left shoulder, feeling it lead the right side into action. Re-create this feeling in your swing and pile on the extra yardage. ***—Rina Ritson***

Wrist Hinge

See how the wrists should hinge when the club is halfway back

By the time the backswing is complete, the left wrist hinges roughly 90 degrees, storing energy to be unleashed when it unhinges through impact. The proper hinging in the backswing is up, creating a right angle between the back of your left thumb and the side of your forearm.

To get the proper feel for the wrist hinge, take your grip and then straighten your right index finger so it's off to the side of the shaft. Then swing the club back. About halfway to the top, the finger should point up to the sky, indicating a 90-degree hinge and helping you build power for the downswing. ***—Martin Hall***

QUICK TIP

Practice with Your Driver

The driver deserves a large chunk—up to 50 percent—of your full-swing practice time. Use it to groove a wider, flatter arc by teeing up a ball, raising the driver about a foot above the ground, and swinging back and forth through the air. This is the sensation you want when hitting the ball, for it guarantees a shallow, powerful angle of attack. *—Mitchell Spearman*

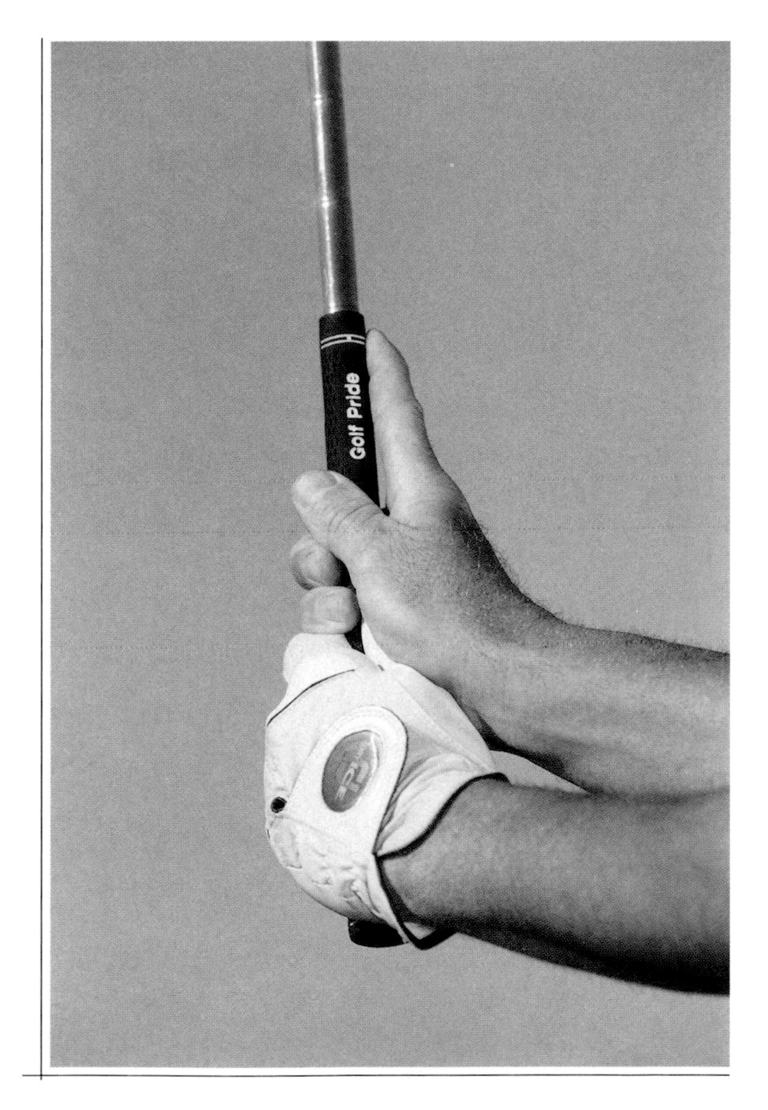
Golf Pride

Stop Slicing

Cure the over-the-top chop with a piece of wood

This drill provides instant feedback and helps cure an outside-to-in swing path.

Place a 2x4 on its narrow edge, not flat. Use a 5-iron and tee up a ball near the front third of the board, exactly one clubhead away. Any closer to the board is too difficult, any farther from it gives you room to cheat. As a visual obstacle, the board should force your club to approach the ball from the inside. If your club strikes the board, you're swinging from out to in and chopping down on the ball, probably hitting a slice. Repeat the drill until you can hit 10 shots without contacting the board, and you'll be on the path to ending your slice. ***—Tom Patri***

CHAPTER 6: STRETCHES AND FITNESS

One-Minute Warm-Up

Don't let a late arrival leave your muscles unprepared

Stretching before a round increases the flexibility and mobility of your muscles. This promotes a bigger body turn and will help you hit longer drives. If you're pressed for time, try these three 20-second exercises.

- **Neck rotations:** Tilt your head to the right side and hold; repeat for the left side.
- **Trunk side bends:** Put your hands on your hips, then bend to each side and hold.
- **Toe touches:** Standing erect, bend at the waist and touch your toes; rise slowly.

Even if you are next on the tee, spending a minute on these key power-producing muscles will help you feel looser and hit the ball longer. ***—Mike McGetrick***

ANTIGUA

Sitting Floor Twist

Make sure your body is ready to swing into action

This is a great stretch to expand your rotational capacity and help you make a better backswing turn for increased distance. It's especially useful early in the season, as muscles tend to adapt to the positions you put them in on a daily basis. If you don't play much in the off-season, they might not be ready once spring comes around.

Sit on the floor, extend your left leg, and cross your right foot so that it's against the outside of your left knee. Brace your left elbow on your right knee and rotate your shoulders as far as you can. Hold for 15 to 20 seconds, then reverse positions and stretch the other way. Work on this twice a day to keep your muscles limber. ***—Mike Malaska***

Daily Double

Two stretches that can be done sitting just about anywhere

Hamstrings: If your hamstrings are tight, you won't be able to bend into the correct posture, and will compensate and lose distance. Sit on the edge of a chair with your back straight. Extend one leg forward and rest your foot on its heel with the toes pointed up, then bend slowly from the hips while keeping your back straight [photo 1]. You'll feel the tension in the hamstring right away. Repeat with the other leg.

Hips: This loosens the hip joints and pelvis so they can provide the support you need to accelerate the club through impact. Sit with your back straight and cross the left leg over the right so that the left ankle sits on the right knee. Gently place your left hand on top of your left knee and let gravity take over, feeling the stretch in your hip [photo 2]. Repeat with the other leg. ***—Laird Small***

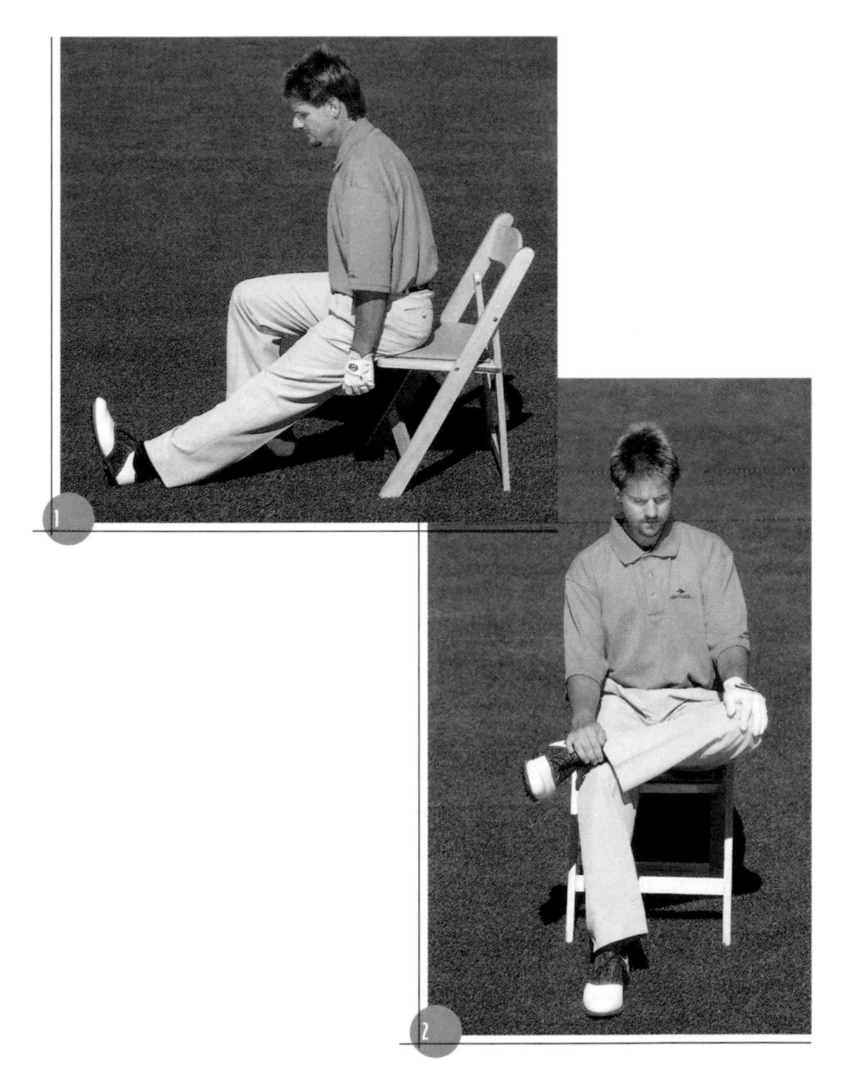
1
2

On-Deck Drill

How to pass the time when the group ahead is teeing off

I call this the "Slugger's Warm-Up," and it will help prepare your body for a bigger turn that will produce more power.

First make a normal swing from start to finish. Then from that finish, swing back making a level, baseball-style swing, rotating your shoulders back as fully as possible and taking the club well past parallel at the top. Now unwind through to a baseball finish to maximize body turn through the swing. If you lose your balance at any point, reduce the size of your turn to the point where you can stay steady. Using a baseball swing to stretch your rotational limits will loosen your shoulders and prepare you to turn farther once it's time to hit the ball. ***—Darrell Kestner***

Side Bends

Do this exercise a few times during the round to stay loose

Stretching properly not only helps you become limber enough to make a powerful swing, but it also reduces tension. Try this stretch during a round to slow a racing mind before an important tee shot.

Grip a club with one hand at either end and hold it over your head. Slowly bend to one side, hold and then bend to the other side [photos 1 and 2]. This increases your ability to make a full rotation so you can step up to the tee and nail your drive. ***—Todd Sones***

1
2